BOOK OF SUPERSTITIOUS STUFF

BOOK OF
Superstitious Stuff

Joanne O'Sullivan

Illustrated by Mike McCoy

imagine!
Publishing
New York
www.imaginebks.com

Text and art copyright © 2010 by Imagine Publishing, Inc.

Published by Imagine Publishing, Inc.
25 Whitman Road, Morganville, NJ 07751

Distributed in the United States of America by
BookMasters Distribution Services, Inc.
30 Amberwood Parkway, Ashland, OH 44805

Distributed in Canada by
BookMasters Distribution Services, Inc.
c/o Jacqueline Gross Associates, 165 Dufferin Street,
Toronto, Ontario, Canada M6K 3H6

Distributed in the United Kingdom by
Publishers Group UK
8 The Arena, Mollison Avenue, Enfield, EN3 7NL, UK

Library of Congress Cataloging-in-Publication Data

O'Sullivan, Joanne.
Book of superstitious stuff / Joanne O'Sullivan.
p. cm.
Includes index.
ISBN 978-1-936140-02-2
1. Superstition. I. Title.
BF1775.O88 2010
001.9′6—dc22
2009035439

Designed by Marc Cheshire
Printed in China
1 3 5 7 9 10 8 6 4 2

For everyone who believes.
Cross your fingers!

Contents

Contents

Introduction

Luck, love, good fortune, and happiness—most of us spend the better part of our lives in their pursuit and the rest our time trying to thwart anything that will stop us from acquiring them. That's what superstitions are all about.

Today we have more education, technology, and data than our superstitious ancestors could ever have dreamed of, all of it pointing to the fact that logic, not superstition, has the answers we're looking for. But that doesn't stop us from walking around a ladder instead of under it, or saying, "knock on wood" when we want to protect something. While some observe superstitions only out of tradition, others are true believers, and still others just don't want to tempt fate. If there's even a slight chance that eating long noodles will let you live longer, some say it's worth a shot. And if garlic over your door keeps evil at bay, why not string some up?

Superstitious?

In a world where so much can be explained through science and rational thought, sometimes it's nice to keep hold of a little mystery. In fact, researchers say that as our connection to beliefs of the past starts to slip away, there are some

THOSE SUPERSTITIOUS AMERICANS

According to a poll conducted by the Associated Press in 2007:

- ▸ 34% of Americans believe in ghosts
- ▸ 19% believe in spells or witchcraft
- ▸ 48% believe in extrasensory perception (ESP)

THOSE SUPERSTITIOUS BRITS

In a survey conducted by Dr. Richard Wiseman at the University of Hertfordshire in 2003:

- ▸ 77% of Brits touch wood for luck
- ▸ 65% cross their fingers for luck
- ▸ 50% avoid walking under ladders
- ▸ 39% believe smashing a mirror will bring bad luck
- ▸ 28% carry a good luck charm
- ▸ 26% believe the number thirteen is bad luck

we stubbornly cling to. The rich, the poor, the educated, the unschooled, and even a military junta—people from all walks of life are superstitious (and you won't believe some of the things people believe).

In this collection of superstitions and their stories, you'll find explanations for some familiar beliefs and discover others you've never heard of. You'll see that everywhere in the world, superstitions are far from dead. In fact, people just keep finding new ways to interpret them. From the curse of the lottery winners to the good feng shui of a McDonald's franchise, old superstitions are keeping pace with the modern world, helping us make sense of all the uncertainty life throws our way.

Are You Feeling Lucky?

HEALTH, wealth, fame, and love . . . they can all be yours if you're lucky. But good luck doesn't just fall into your lap. There are certain things you must do to attract it while simultaneously avoiding luck of the bad variety. There are countless superstitions about good and bad luck in cultures all over the world. Lucky numbers, lucky colors, lucky days, lucky charms—and for every one of them, there's an unlucky equivalent. Good luck keeping track of them all!

NUMBERS GAME

It's no coincidence that the lottery—the ultimate game of chance—is based on numbers. Ever since humans invented numbers, they've had superstitions about which ones are good luck and which are bad. Sure you've heard of unlucky thirteen, but did you know you should be careful of three, four, and seventeen as well? When you add it all up, you can't really count to ten without running into some misfortune.

Three Is a Magic Number

They say, "Third time's a charm." But then again, "Bad things come in threes." The number three has been considered a spiritual number since ancient times. There were three main Egyptian and Hindu gods. In Christianity, God has three incarnations: the Father, the Son, and the Holy Spirit. Three often turns up in traditional fairy tales, too: the three bears, three little pigs, and three wishes granted by magical creatures, for instance. Counting to three is often a precursor to a surprise, and three shows up in sports, too: three strikes you're out, three hockey goals equals a hat trick. It's an old gambler's superstition that if you're having bad luck at the table, get up, turn around three times, and go back. Your luck will have reversed itself, and you'll be a winner.

Devilish Digits

According to the Bible, 666 is the devil's number. Like the number thirteen, 666 is frequently absent from hotels, hospitals, airline-flight schedules, and street addresses, because it gives people the creeps. Horror and suspense movies such as *The Omen* have only played up the superstition.

When a San Francisco taxi driver was assigned to drive a cab with the number 666, he had the vehicle blessed at a local church. But he said that he still had bad luck after having received the number and asked to have it switched. (The commission in charge of cab licenses said "no.")

Workers at a law firm in Birmingham, England said that their office—in an old Victorian home with the street address 666—is cursed and haunted, and they refused to work late. One coworker was found dead at her desk after working late, and several others have experienced misfortune. The employees believe that the office address is to blame.

Ronald and Nancy Regan shared those sentiments about the

I could have sworn I pressed "4."

spooky street address. When they left the White House, they bought a home with the address 666 St. Cloud Road, but they had the address changed to 668.

When the date 6-6-06 rolled around some felt panic, while others—like those in the town of Hell, Michigan—made light of the date. They had a big party.

The Elevator Doesn't Stop
at the Fourth Floor . . .

. . . Because there is no fourth floor! The Chinese word for "four" rhymes with the word for "death," so in China, most buildings over three stories tall skip four in the numbering. (Of course there is a fourth floor, but it's numbered five). In buildings with a fourth floor, the apartments on that floor are usually the cheapest and occupied by foreigners.

Complaints from superstitious parents in Shanghai recently

led to the recall by one cab company of all taxis with the number four in the license plate. A ride in a cab bearing the unlucky number would ruin their children's chances of getting a good grade on their exams, the parents said.

Lucky 7

Like the number three, seven has a long history as a number with spiritual significance: there are seven days in the week, and the seventh is the day of rest. In Japan, there are seven gods of good luck. In ancient times, it was believed that there were seven planets and seven seas. The seventh son of a seventh son was supposed to be an extraordinary person.

A Texas baby made news by being born on July 7, 2007 at 7:57 AM, weighing seven pounds, seven ounces. On this same day, couples all over the world arranged to be married, some at 7:00 AM and some at 7:00 PM. One Illinois couple married on that day gave out lottery tickets to their guests.

The Ritz Carlton Hotel in New York offered a special wedding package for seventy-seven guests, including a seven-tier cake, seven diamonds for the bride, and seven nights in the hotel, all for $77,777. In Japanese tradition, July 7 is the Festival of Tanabata, which celebrates the Japanese myth of two stars who were lovers and were only allowed meet once a year—on the seventh night of the seventh month.

Eight Is Great

In Chinese, the word for "eight" is pronounced very similarly to the word for "wealth and fortune," so it's considered one of the luckiest numbers.

When Beijing was chosen to host the Summer Olympics in 2008, the organizers made sure the games opened on 08/08/08 at 8:08 PM for extra good luck. The games were thought to have gone extremely well, and China won a record number of medals. The same date was also very much in demand for weddings in China and the US. An online wedding registry reported that weddings for August 8, 2008 were up 400% over the same date the previous year.

In China, car owners go to great lengths to get a license plate featuring the number eight. A license plate with a four is considered very bad luck and may lead to traffic accidents, but one with an eight is lucky and thought to help provide protection on the road. Such plates were in such high demand that the government started auctioning them off. Bids are often twice the cost of an average car and up to twenty-times the yearly salary of an average Chinese worker in the rural areas. The more eights on the plate, the better. A license plate with six eights recently went for the equivalent of $130,000. The highest price paid for a plate in Hong Kong was $1.7 million Hong Kong dollars. Fancy plates aren't just for the superstitions—they're a status symbol, showing you can afford them. You can also get a lucky eight for your cell phone—for a price. Numbers heavy on the eights can go for up to $2,000.

Elevenses

If you make a wish at 11:11, it's supposed to come true, says a more recent superstition of unknown origin. Celebrity model and actress Paris Hilton says she follows this tradition. Some say that wishes will come true at any minute on the clock when all the numbers are the same: 2:22 or 3:33 for example.

Unlucky Thirteen

It's the most universally feared number. But why? Some say the superstition started with Norse mythology and the story of Balder's death. Twelve gods were having dinner when the evil Loki—the thirteenth guest— turned up, bringing with him a piece of mistletoe that killed the beloved god Balder. The Bible says there were also thirteen at the Last

Supper, the night before Jesus was killed. This doomed thirteen-guest dinner party history led to the superstition that if thirteen people sit down together to eat, one would die within the year. (Sometimes it was said to be the first to leave the table.) Because of this superstition, the Savoy Hotel in London began to offer parties of thirteen extra help to overcome potential bad luck. Since the 1920s, all parties of thirteen are rounded up with the addition of Kaspar, a three-foot-tall black Art Deco sculpture of a cat that occupies the fourteenth seat. In nineteenth century France, superstitious people would hire a *quatorzieme* (fourteenth) to join their table, if needed.

In New York during the 1880s, a group called the Thirteen Club decided to tempt fate. They met on the 13th of each month dining at thirteen tables of thirteen guests each. Several US presidents and other luminaries were members of the club, which continued for over two decades without losing members to suspicious circumstances.

A Belgian airline had to paint an additional circle on their logo after an outcry from passengers when they noticed the number thirteen featured on it. Some airlines have no gate thirteen or row thirteen on the plane, and it's quite common for hotels to have no thirteenth floor. (They have one, of course, it's just not numbered that way.) In Italy, thirteen is not a number you can play in the lottery. In Palmerston North, New Zealand, the town council eliminated street numbers between eleven and fifteen. It seems that houses numbered thirteen and those next to them were sitting empty due to superstition. Municipalities in other areas have stopped issuing the number on new properties, and real estate agents in many countries report that a house numbered thirteen is more difficult to sell.

American horror writer Stephen King is very superstitious

You know what? I think I'll wait for the next flight.

about the number thirteen. When writing, he won't stop on page thirteen or on any number that contains the number thirteen in it or which when added together equals thirteen.

However, in 2009, thirteen women who worked on the thirteenth floor of a building in Edmonton, Alberta won $49 million in the lottery when they pooled their money to purchase the winning ticket. And an English baby born thirteen minutes after the thirteenth hour on Friday the 13th helped his parents to overcome their superstition. The baby—who weighed six pounds, seven ounces (which adds up to thirteen) was the luckiest thing that ever happened to his parents, they said. (Just wait till he turns thirteen!)

The Edge of Seventeen

In Italy, the number seventeen is considered to be unlucky because of the Roman numerals for the number. If you switch around XVII, and change them to VIXI, it means, "He has lived." in Latin. It's often inscribed on tombstones, so the number is said to tempt death to one's door. The numbers one and seven are also said to look like a hanged man and a gallows, also leading to bad luck. German airline Lufthansa skips row seventeen in its seating to honor this superstition. Delta Airlines skips both row thirteen and seventeen in certain aircraft.

The Jury's Still Out

Do numbers really make a difference in the way we live our lives? In 2006, a juror was booted from a high-profile murder trial in Washington, DC because she insisted on factoring in the birthdates of the accused and victim in her decision instead of just relying on the evidence.

Bollywood filmmakers often rely on numerology to decide on the title of a movie, changing the spelling to create a numerologically lucky title. (Each letter has a number value in numerology.) They'll also add numbers to the title to increase its chances of success.

That's Odd

When giving a gift of money in China, it should never be for an odd-numbered amount.

Star Trek fans have a long-held superstition that even-numbered *Star Trek* movies are good and the odd ones are bad.

When giving flowers as a gift in Russia, you should always have an odd number—even numbers are for funeral flowers.

LAWS OF ATTRACTION

If superstitions are to be believed, love, luck, power, money, and happiness can be yours if you only know how to attract them. While you're at it though, you're going to have to do some work to keep their opposites at bay.

Nunsense

Most everyone has heard the superstition that you must knock on wood to keep bad luck away. But in Italy, there's a twist. Nuns are considered to bring bad luck, so when you pass a nun on the street, you should touch iron to reverse the luck or turn to the next passerby and say, "Your nun!" to transfer the bad luck to him or her.

Offended by the implication of this age-old practice, a group of Italian nuns formed a band called Sister Act in 1999 to record a rap album that countered the superstition. The album's single, "Your Nun, Touch Iron," won third prize in a national song contest. Yet, low and behold, a group of rapping nuns with a hot 12-track CD to their credit isn't enough to dispel this practice.

This place is fishy!

The Feng Shui Way

Feng shui, which means "wind and water" in Chinese, is an ancient system that attracts luck and prosperity and ensures the positive flow of energy through the proper arrangement of the home or workplace, or the proper choice of clothing. Some consider feng shui a legitimate science, others a superstition. It was even outlawed during the Cultural Revolution when the communist government was trying to rid the country of old customs. According to feng shui principles, living near a winding river is good because it invites good energy flow, but living near a hospital invites bad energy because it attracts illness. The southeast corner of the home is the wealth center, so it should be painted red if wealth is to be attracted.

While feng shui was once only practiced in China, it became very trendy in Western countries around the turn of the 21st century—so much so, that even McDonald's and other fastfood franchises started hiring feng shui experts to redesign their restaurants. Disneyland also consulted with feng shui experts before building a Hong Kong Disneyland. Yet somehow, this trend hasn't done much for the positive flow of the long lines at these establishments.

When one Taiwanese gambler lost $2 million at the Venetian Hotel and Casino in Las Vegas, he sued the casino for thwarting his winning streak with bad feng shui. According to his complaint, the hotel made a forty-inch diameter hole in his hotel room wall, covered it with a black cloth, and put two white towels outside his door. ("Draping" of black and white cloths signifies a death in the family.) They also turned on fans without alerting him. The casino settled with the man out of court.

In Japan, a popular series of feng shui books led to a nationwide bathroom cleaning frenzy, which took up news time and became the theme of several television shows. The books claimed that a sparkling clean bathroom was the key to attracting luck and advised people not only to scrub the bowl, but also to polish the floor and maintain a positive attitude while performing these tasks. Many who adhered to the advise reported that they met their dream partner, won the lottery, or finally got pregnant after getting their bathrooms in order.

The Bank of China's seventy-story Hong Kong headquarters aroused concern in feng shui believers when it opened in 1990. Its sharp sides were said to resemble daggers, and the antennae on top of the building look like chopsticks sticking straight up (a symbol associated with death). Many of those within sight distance of the building hung mirrors outside their homes in order to reflect the bad luck back onto the bank.

Under(wear) Pressure

When diplomacy seemed doomed to failure, a Canadian women's group called Panties for Peace decided to try superstition to wrest the Burmese (Myanmar) military junta

The Boxer Rebellion this wasn't.

from power. The oppressive regime had resisted international efforts to bring peace and a democratic government to the Southeast Asian country for decades. PFP members suggested a new approach. Group members found out that

Burmese men believe that touching a woman's underwear will rob them of their power, so they began emptying out their underwear drawers and sending the contents to the Myanmar embassy in Ottawa. The women taped or glued pictures of the military dictators to the panties so that the leaders were "touching" them. Women in Australia, Singapore, Brazil, the Philippines, and countries across Europe also joined in the effort. The group's organizers called it a form of nonviolent social change that let ordinary women register their opposition to the junta.

The junta's leaders are notoriously superstitious, subscribing to a traditional belief system called *yadaya*. They have forced farmers to grow sunflowers because they're supposed to ward off enemies. They are also said to have Ouija boards present at official functions.

Luring in Lady Luck

In the *hoodoo* tradition of the American South, you can attract luck with a mojo bag—a small bag made from red flannel containing an odd number (usually 3, 5, 7, 9, or 13) of items such as John the Conqueror root (used by gamblers to attract luck), a lodestone (used for attraction), a pair of dice, or a rabbit's foot. To attract love, a bag (called a "nation sack" if it's carried by a woman) might contain two lodestones treated with an oil. A mojo bag has to be "dressed" with candle smoke, alcohol, or bodily fluids in order to become effective.

In Japan, students believe that eating a Kit Kat candy bar before an exam will bring luck. The Japanese name for the candy—Kitto Katto—sounds very similar to "kitto kattsu," which means "win without fail" in Japanese. Nestle, the company that makes the candy bar, has taken advantage of this fortunate translation by adding cherry blossoms to its Japanese Kit Kat packaging—a symbol that is also linked to success in college.

YOUR LUCKY DAY

There are 365 reasons each year for you to be superstitious. Each day brings new potential for you to test your luck by traveling on a Tuesday or getting your hair cut on a Wednesday. Watch your back as March 15th approaches, and whatever you do, don't eat squid on New Year's Day.

From Day One

Banging pots and pans or making loud noises on New Year's Eve started out as a way to scare evil spirits away so that they don't follow you into the new year. In Turkey, people put on new red underwear moments before the clock strikes midnight on New Year's so that they'll start a new year with good luck. Each December, top Turkish underwear companies report a 20% increase in sales.

On the Scottish New Year's Eve (known as Hogmanay), people compete to be the "first footer"—the first person to cross

Unfortunately, this year's first footer was trampled to death by feet numbers two through twenty-eight.

a friend's threshold in the new year with gifts for good luck. One Scottish man who was attempting a first foot was later jailed because he had entered the wrong house and acted unruly when asked to leave.

In China, sweeping your doorstep on New Year's Eve will sweep away the bad luck of the previous year, but you shouldn't do it on New Year's Day because that will sweep away the prosperity of the new year. In Thailand, people throw water on each other in the streets on New Years'. (Originally, it was holy water, but now it's more like a water fight). In Costa Rica, it's common to put water in a pan on New Year's Eve, and then throw it over your shoulder, signifying that the bad things of the past are behind you. In the Dominican Republic, if you walk around outside with your suitcase on New Year's Eve, it's said the new year will bring you travel. In many German towns, family members gather at midnight to watch a movie called *Dinner for One*.

In the Southern states of the US, eating black-eyed peas and collard greens is said to bring good luck in the new year. In Mexico and other Latin American countries, you eat twelve grapes on New Year's Eve and make a wish for the new year as you eat each one. In Chinese tradition, noodles on New Year's will bring a long life and steamed rice cakes will bring good luck. Eating squid will bring bad luck (it means you'll lose your job).

Never on a Monday?

In Jamaica, it's considered bad luck to get married on a Monday.

Tuesday is considered an unlucky day in several Mediterranean cultures. In Spain, there's a saying, "En martes, ni te cases ni te embarques," which means, "On Tuesday, neither get married nor begin a journey." While many cultures consider Friday the 13th to be unlucky, in Greece Tuesday the

13th is an inauspicious day. In India (especially parts of the south), it's bad luck to open a business on a Tuesday. On the other hand, in Jewish tradition, Tuesday is considered a good day because in the story of creation, it's mentioned twice that God found this day to be good. The other days were only said to be good once, except Monday, which was not said to be good at all.

Wednesday is considered a day of bad luck in Islamic culture, and people refrain from getting their hair cut on that day.

In India, it's bad luck to begin a journey on a Thursday.

In Medieval England, Friday was associated with bad luck because it was the day on which executions were carried out, thus earning it the nickname Hangman's Day. In most European cultures, Friday is considered to be the unluckiest day of the week.

Saturday was considered the only day to baptize a child in medieval England: choose any other day and the child would die. Bad luck would also come to those who worked on a Sunday.

The Unluckiest Day of the Year

In many Western cultures, even the least superstitious people, are a little cautious when the 13th of the month falls on a Friday. True believers barely step out of the house on the day. In fact, so many people are afraid of Friday the 13th that one psychologist coined a named for the fear of it: *paraskevidekatriaphobia*. According to the Stress Management Center and Phobia Institute, paraskevidekatriaphobia costs businesses hundreds of millions in losses each year from worker "sick days," loss of sales, and drops in travel reservations. Even famed British Prime Minister Winston Churchill and President Franklin D. Roosevelt wouldn't travel on the day. Roosevelt went so far as to reschedule travel on the 13th to

11:50 PM on the 12th or 12:10 AM on the 14th. Even in death he avoided the day. He died on Thursday April 12, 1945.

So how did Friday the 13th earn its unfortunate reputation? No one knows for sure. Some say that it's because Jesus was killed on a Friday. Others say that it was a Friday the 13th (October 13, 1307) when King Phillip of France slaughtered the Knights Templar (of *DaVinci Code* fame) who were said to be the protectors of the Holy Grail. More likely it is because the number thirteen (see page 23) and Fridays (see page 42) both are known to be unlucky. So the combination of the two is bound to be bad.

According to the British Medical Journal, hospital admittance due to traffic accidents increases by up to 25% on Fridays the 13th. On the other hand, few people schedule surgeries on this day. And a Dutch study revealed that fewer

The waiting room of doom.

accidents happen on Friday the 13th. In fact, researchers concluded that more accidents happen on Monday the 27th than any other day. So, why aren't we all superstitious about Mondays the 27th!?

How do you prevent bad luck on Friday the 13th? If you were born on a Friday the 13th you don't have to do anything—according to one superstition, there's a kind of cosmic immunity card for those born on the day and it's actually lucky. So, even if it's bad luck to be born on a Friday, you're okay on the 13th. Go figure!

Bad Things That Really Happened on Friday 13th

A plane crash on Friday, October 13, 1972 killed fifteen members of an Uruguayan soccer team and left twenty-nine others in their group stranded in the Andes Mountains for over two months. They had to resort to cannibalism to live.

On Friday, October 13, 1989 there was a stock market "mini-crash."

On Friday the 13th in 1984, Arkansas resident Terry Wells

flipped his pickup truck into a ditch and went into a coma-like state. Bad luck? On Friday the 13th, 2003, he "woke up," in what doctors called a 1 in 300 million chance of his brain "rewiring" itself.

Apollo 13 was launched on April 11, 1970 but ran into problems two days later on April 13th and the lunar landing had to be aborted. This mission made famous the catchphrase, "Houston, we have a problem."

Things That Didn't Happen On Friday the 13th

One longstanding urban legend about Friday the 13th concerns the HMS Friday, which is said to have set sail from Portsmouth, England on a Friday the 13th with a man called Friday at the helm, only to disappear completely. According to the story, the famous insurer Lloyds of London stopped insuring boats launched on Friday the 13th because of this misfortune. The Royal Maritime Museum reports that the rumor is just poppycock—no such ship ever existed.

The 2004 Summer Olympics held in Athens, Greece opened on Friday, August 13, 2004. Unless you count that god-awful dance number during the closing ceremonies, nothing really bad happened as a result of the unfortunate start date.

Friday the 13th Facts

There is at least one Friday the 13th each year and sometimes as many as three. The Friday the 13th "triple threat" only comes around every eleven years.

Friday the 13th is said to be doubly unlucky when it falls on a Good Friday.

Cuban President Fidel Castro, British Prime Minister Margaret Thatcher, and the famous American outlaw Butch Cassidy were all born on Friday the 13th.

Beware the Ides of March!

For some Americans, a sense of dread grows as the fateful day approaches: April 15th—tax day. For ancient Romans, March 15 had a similar effect: the ides of March (and of all other months) was the midpoint of the month, a day to pay up for any debts you owed. Thanks to Shakespeare, we remember this day as the day that Julius Caesar's debts came due. He was murdered by his political rivals, paying his debts to the Romans with blood. Once Shakespeare wrote the lines, "Beware the Ides of March!" he sealed March 15's fate as an ominous day forever. In fact, there are "ides" in each month of the Roman calendar—it simply meant the middle of the month, when bills were due. The ides fell on the 15th of the month for three months and on the 13th of the month in the others. Since Shakespeare's time, the Ides of March has been associated with betrayal, and the cautious

We can't attack on Tuesday, you moron! Mercury's in retrograde.

are advised to "watch your back" when it rolls around.

Nancy Reagan's Astrologer

First Lady Nancy Reagan took a lot of heat for her belief

in astrology. Not surprising considering that her astrologer, Joan Quigley, claimed that she, "practically ran the White House." Quigley advised the Reagan's on auspicious days and times (down to the second) for making Supreme Court nominations, traveling, and important international meetings. When Regan made one nomination according to her time schedule, the nominee was unanimously confirmed.

When a new prime minister was elected in Nepal in 1998, he refused to be sworn in on a Monday because it was the last day of the year in the Nepalese calendar, and so is considered inauspicious for starting new ventures.

COLOR ME LUCKY

What color would you wear to a funeral? A wedding? Depending on where you live, your choice of color isn't just a matter of taste. It could be the difference between a lucky life or impending doom.

51

Green

In the world of racecars, green has always been considered an unlucky color. The superstition dates to the 1920s when the driver of a green car was killed in an on-track accident. Since then, racecar drivers avoid green cars and fans in the stands don't wear green on race day. Drivers are not even supposed to speak to anyone wearing green on race day. Famed racecar driver Mario Andretti is said never to sign autographs in green ink.

In the theater, the green room (where actors wait before coming out on to the stage) should never been painted green. Some actors avoid green costumes or props. Some say this superstition evolved from the death of the 19th-century French actor and playwright Molière. It's said he was wearing green on stage when he expired. In England, green is associated with fairies and mischief, and therefore should be avoided.

Meanwhile, green is considered a sacred color in Islam. It's said that green symbolized the oasis, which was critical for life to continue in desert cultures. Mosques often feature green onion domes. In China, green is considered auspicious because of its association with growth.

In ancient Egypt, green was considered to be a magical color with sacred energy that could be used for either good or bad. Historians believe this association came from the link between green and plant growth and life. Green scarab beetle amulets were sometimes placed over the hearts of mummies and green stone amulets were sometimes put into their hands to ensure safe transit to the afterlife.

Red

Red is the color of good fortune in China. Brides wear red, and on holidays, monetary gifts are given out in red envelopes. Red is said to protect against evil spirits, and it's also the color of happiness. Red lanterns and banners are hung at celebrations. In India, red is the color of purity, and it's the most common color for wedding gowns. A bride also wears a red *tikka* (dot) on her head for her wedding.

Red and white are worn at funerals in certain African ethnic groups, but it would be quite offensive to wear red at a Chinese funeral. In Japan and Korea, you should never write a person's name in red ink or the person will die.

Golfer Tiger Woods always wears a red shirt on the Sunday of any golf tournament. His mother is from Thailand where red is considered a lucky color, and he had good luck wearing it on Sundays early in his career.

Blue

In Greece, blue is thought to ward off the evil eye. In Morocco, a blue dot is painted on the ear of a groom for the same reason. In ancient Egypt, it was considered the color of fidelity and truth, which eventually evolved into the European wedding tradition of brides wearing "something blue" to show their faithfulness. In the American South, the roofs of porches are often painted blue. While some say this is to signify the sky, others say it's "haint paint"—a color that's intended to scare off haints or ghosts.

It's considered unlucky for actors to wear blue on stage, but its negativity can be reversed by wearing the color silver with it. In Thailand, blue is the color associated with Friday. In Iran, blue is the color of mourning.

Black

In many cultures, black is the color of death and is the only choice for funerals and mourning periods. In stories and movies, it's a common convention that "bad guys wear black." In Thailand, it's bad luck to wear black to a wedding.

Can I interest you in something a little, um, lighter?

Purple

Actors are advised not to wear purple on opening night, and it's bad luck to send purple flowers to a performer on the first night of a run. In the Philippines, girls of marriageable age should not wear purple or they will never marry. Purple was the color of royalty in medieval Europe. The colors of Mardi Gras—the mid-winter carnival celebration held in areas of the US once occupied by France—are green, gold, and purple. The purple is said to represent justice, the green represents faith, and the gold is for power. Purple is the color of mourning for widows in Thailand.

White

While white symbolizes purity in European culture and is worn by brides, in East Asian countries, it's the color of death and is worn at funerals. In India, widows wear white, not black.

Yellow

In Spain, yellow is considered an unlucky color. In Tibet, yellow silk umbrellas are a common gift for bestowing good luck. In Hindu culture, yellow is the color of truth and immortality. In China, it's a royal color. Chinese emperors were seated in yellow chairs and their armies carried yellow silk flags. Brides wore yellow in ancient Rome. In Thailand, it's considered good luck to wear yellow on Mondays in honor of the King, who was born on a Monday. For some Thai companies, wearing yellow on Monday is a requirement.

Orange

Buddhist monks wear orange robes, so it's considered a sacred color in Buddhist countries. Orange is associated with good luck in China, so oranges are a common gift, especially at New Year's. In India, orange or saffron is associated with Hinduism and it's also the color of celebration. Marigold garlands are used at all festive occasions.

UTTER NONSENSE

Even if you don't have the proper charms or amulets, you may be able to avert disaster and draw fortune with just a few well-chosen words.

Knock Wood

Chances are you've said, "Knock on wood" or "Touch wood," countless times in your life without even knowing why. In many cultures, it's the expression used to make sure that current good luck continues or that bad luck stays away. Some speculate that the custom has its origins in pagan times when benevolent spirits were thought to live in trees, so touching or knocking on wood would bring their good blessing to whatever situation was being discussed. Others say, however, that the tradition can't be traced any further back than a 19th-century children's game similar to tag in which players tagged each other and said "touch wood" or "touch iron."

Going Off Script

You can look at it two ways: Either actors are very superstitious or they're great followers of tradition. One of the best-known luck-bringing expressions in the world comes from the theater—break a leg. While it's now used to grant luck before endeavors of every kind, it started in the theater. The phrase only seems to date back to the early 20th century, and there are several theories on how it started. It could be that telling an actor good luck with attract the evil eye (see page 117), so saying "break a leg" would be a protective charm. Or it could be meant to encourage an energetic performance.

Actors everywhere who perform *Macbeth* refer to the play as "that Scottish play," because it's considered bad luck to utter the name of the gloomy play in a theater. If the name of the play is accidentally said, the speaker should leave the theater, turn around three times counterclockwise, spit, utter a swear word, and then knock on the door to be let back in. Another version of the superstition says that you can reverse the bad luck by saying, "Thrice around the circle bound, Evil sink into the ground."

Geez, all I said was, "Good luck with Macbeth *tonight."*

While no one can pinpoint the exact source of the superstition, it seems that the play has brought bad luck from the beginning.

One actor murdered another on stage and dozens of people were trampled at performance in 19th-century New York. The actor Laurence Olivier was nearly crushed by a weight when he was acting in the lead part. Some say that the chant uttered by the "weird sisters" in the play is a curse in itself. Others say that the macabre nature of the play just leaves people a little more superstitious.

In a 1957 outdoor production of the play in Bermuda, Charlton Heston (who was playing the lead) was riding a horse on stage when he had to exit, writhing in pain. It seems that his tights had somehow been soaked in kerosene, and the friction between the horse, his legs, and the tights had caused burns on his thighs and groin area. Later that same night, a sudden gust of wind blew flames from the set's torches into the audience who fled the amphitheater, causing a stampede.

Whistling

Superstitions about whistling abound in cultures all over the world. In addition to the well-known admonition of afore-mentioned superstitious actors (never whistle in a theater—it brings bad luck), there's the Russian superstition about whistling in your home: If you do it, you'll whistle away your money.

In Japan, superstition dictates that you shouldn't whistle at night or you'll summon up spirits.

There's a long-standing sailor's superstition against whistling. It's said to whistle up ill winds. Some even say that the sailors brought the whistling superstition to the theater. Since they

Yeah, listen, I'm gonna need you over here in Devonshire.
We got ourselves a whistler.

knew how to work with ropes, they were sometimes employed to work backstage, hoisting curtains and backdrops. According to an old English superstition, "A whistling woman, a crowing hen starts the Devil from his den."

In addition to the no whistling rule, performers at the legendary Apollo Theater in Harlem avoid eating peanuts backstage. No one really knows the origin of the superstition, except that it was passed down to younger performers by Moms Mabley, the legendary vaudeville actress who performed there for decades.

According to news reports, Axl Rose, former lead singer of the band Guns 'n' Roses, will not play in towns that begin with the letter M because he thinks the letter is cursed.

Jinx!
In Greece, if two friends say the same thing at the same time,

it's an omen that they will get in a fight. To avoid it, they should both say "touch red" and touch a red item immediately. In the US, children sometimes say "jinx" when two inadvertently say the same thing at the same time, but in England they say "snap."

All's Quiet

Among police officers everywhere, saying, "It's quiet," is known to bring on incidents of mass pandemonium. As soon as "the q word," is spoken, police dispatchers are flooded with calls, officers report.

Words of Warning

In rural Egypt, women customarily say, "Watch out!" before throwing hot water down the sink in order to alert the jinn (genie) who might be living in the pipe to get out of the way. In Ireland, there's a similar custom. People would say, "Take care," or "Away with yourself from the water," before throw-

Sure is quiet out here tonight.

ing dirty water out the door in the darkness in case the "good people" (fairies) were passing by. If they were inadvertently hit with dirty water, cows might stop giving milk or some other misfortune might come to the home.

Something Bunny

In the small town of Portland in Dorset, England, saying the word "rabbit" can instantly stop a conversation. The area is known for its quarries, and rabbit burrows near quarries have long been responsible for landslides that can bury miners. Sighting a rabbit near a quarry would bring work to a halt for the day until the safety of the area had been determined. Even uttering the word "rabbit" was said to bring bad luck. Instead, the animals are referred to as "furry things" or "underground mutton."

When the movie *Wallace & Gromit: Curse of the Were-Rabbit* was released in England, the producers created a special poster for the movie out of deference to the local superstition. Instead of mentioning the film's title, the posters just said, "Something bunny is going on."

Rabbits are the subject of another English verbal superstition. If you say "rabbit, rabbit, white rabbit" on the first day of each month before saying any other words that day, you'll have a lucky month. Variations of the practice include saying "bunny, bunny, hop, hop" or "rabbit, rabbit, rabbit" on the first night of the full moon instead of the first of the month. In another version, you say three "rabbits" before bed on the last night of the month and three "hares" upon waking up in the new month, or saying "black rabbit" at night and "white rabbit" when waking up.

ROAD RULES

Leaving one's home is fraught with perils—especially if you're setting out on a long journey. To avoid disaster, it's often necessary to take a few peculiar precautions.

Ready or Not

In colonial America, there was an old superstition that if you left the house on a journey and the first thing you saw was a woman or a cat, you'd meet misfortune on your journey. If the woman was barefoot, you do best to turn around and go back because something really bad would happen. Another version of the superstition said that that if you saw a squirrel crossing the road just after leaving the house, you should note its direction. If it went left you'd have bad luck on your journey; if it went right, you'd have a successful trip. There's no note as to what would happen if the squirrel went straight ahead or ran toward you.

In Ukraine, you should observe a few minutes of silence in your home before leaving for a journey. In Russia, it's bad luck to return to your house to get something if you've just left. If you must do so, look in the mirror while you're in the house to get your luck back before leaving again. In Turkey, it's considered bad luck to turn and look behind you once you've left on a journey.

On the Road

As far back as ancient Greece, garnets and emeralds were carried in the pockets of travelers who could afford them because they were said to bring good luck.

In medieval Europe, sleigh bells or bells on horses were originally meant to drive away evil spirits that might attack on the road.

Around the 18th century, Catholics in Europe started carrying or wearing a medal featuring St. Christopher (whose name means "Christ-bearer") while they traveled. He was known as the patron saint of travelers because he was said to have carried Jesus safely across a river. Among Catholics, it was once common to start a journey by saying, "St. Christopher be our guide." Numerous stories exist of St. Christopher medals saving lives: deflecting bullets, getting caught on tree limbs and thus preventing fatal falls, and other "miracles" (no telling how true these stories are).

When the car became a common means of transportation, the custom of carrying a charm or amulet was translated into using the dashboard or rearview mirror for your good-luck saint or pair of fuzzy dice.

Out of This World Superstitions

Among American astronauts, there is a preflight ritual card game that must take place before suiting up and heading onto the launch pad. Before each launch, the astronauts are always presented a cake and have their picture taken with it, but the cake is never eaten. Inside the living quarters of the module, there are stickers from each previous mission. The astronauts must slap the sticker from any mission that he or she has taken part in before blasting off.

Russian cosmonauts always leave red carnations at a memorial honoring those who have died either in training or on missions. They later visit the office of one of the dead cosmonauts (which has been preserved as a shrine), sign his guest book, and ask his ghost's permission to fly. They get a haircut the day the rocket is rolled onto the pad and put coins on the rocket's track as it's rolled out so that the coin will be flattened by the weight of it (that is said to bring good luck). The night before launch, they always watch the same movie: *White Sun of the Desert*. On the day of the launch, they drink champagne, sing a song called "The Green Grass of My Home," and ride a bus decorated with horseshoes to the launch pad. They urinate on the right rear wheel of the bus when they get out. They hang a talisman—kind of like a rear-window ornament—in the capsule. When they are finally in orbit, it floats around the cabin.

Traveler's Rest

In Turkey, it's considered bad luck to stay at a hotel or rest stop located at a three-way intersection. Sleeping near the side of a road is also a bad idea. It's thought that the devil will come and paralyze you. Never mind what a car would do to you. . . .

While feng shui believers can exercise control over luck and flow of *chi* within their own home, it's harder to do so on the road. It's now possible to buy a feng shui travel kit so that hotel rooms will not bring bad luck on the road. The kits—sold online by various feng shui masters—include items such as incense and candles, as well as instructions for applying feng shui principles to travel accommodations.

Setting Sail

Sailors are known to be a superstitious lot. Among the best-known sailor's superstitions is the one against whistling. The belief is said to be tied to the devil, who has a strong association with whistling. Whistling at sea would make the devil believe the sailors were mocking him, it was thought, and so he would exact vengeance by blasting the boat with "ill winds."

A Scottish town that hosts an annual boating festival recently imposed a month-long ban on whistling to ensure that the event would take place under sunny skies with favorable wind conditions.

Sailors dread anything having to do with the left-hand side. Getting on and off a ship was always done with the right foot first (putting you best foot forward). While a black cat is trouble in most circumstances, on a ship it was thought to be a good omen. Bananas on a boat, however, were thought to bring bad luck.

Gold earrings were said to protect a sailor from a watery grave. In Scotland, sailors were required to wear them so that if they washed ashore after drowning, the earring could be sold to pay for a funeral.

"Christening" a ship with a champagne bottle broken over the bow is a long-standing tradition said to bring good luck. If the bottle fails to break, it's considered a bad omen. The Duchess of Cornwall failed to break the bottle when launching a luxury cruise ship in 2007, and three weeks later passengers on the ship suddenly fell victim to a mysterious stomach illness. A ship that was unsuccessfully christened in 2000 broke down just eighteen hours later.

A Blessing
or a Curse

FROM ghoulies and ghosties and long-leggedy beasties, and things that go bump in the night, Good Lord, deliver us!" Some modern-day folks have alarms to protect them from such things, but then again, the evil eye can't be thwarted by a security system. If you're superstitious, keeping evil and misfortune away—or directing it toward your enemies—is just as important as it ever was, and it requires more than a code and the touch of a few buttons. It takes charms, amulets, incantations, and the occasional witch doctor.

CHARMED I'M SURE

Lucky charms (the objects, not the cereal) are common in every culture the world over. Some of them—such as the horseshoe or the lucky penny—are widely recognized, while others are quite personal (see the following story on Mark McGwire). Whether they work or not, those who use them would rather not tempt fate.

Charm Offensive

Natural talent, years of practice and discipline—that's what sports announcers would have you believe goes into making the world's most successful athletes. But if you ask the athletes themselves, you may find out that they give more credit to their lucky charms. Professional athletes may be among the most superstitious people in the world, but they're certainly not picky about what they turn to for luck. A certain pair of tube socks, a battered old mitt—these humble "charms" could mean the difference between victory and defeat.

The great basketball player Michael Jordan always wore his University of North Carolina team shorts under his Chicago Bulls uniform. US Olympic swimmer Gary Hall wore his lucky robe and trunks to events rather than team gear and ended up with a surprising gold medal. One African Cup of Nations soccer player is said to have played with an elephant's tooth in his shoe. And rumor has it that that US

*Nielsen's choice of good luck charms deflated his
team's chances for a victory.*

baseball batter Mark McGwire wore the same athletic sup-
porter from his high school days into the major leagues.

In Swaziland, people can hire witch doctors called *sangoma*

So, as your doctor, I suggest you kick the ball.

to create *muti*, a magic charm that can be used on various objects to bring luck or send a curse to enemies. In 2008, the brand-new $600,000 Astroturf in the country's only stadium had to be replaced because it had been cut and burned in places (mostly near the goals) because athletes (or their supporters) had put muti underneath it. One muti was a list of players' names and another was a dead chicken. It's believed that the muti were intended to bring defeat to opposing teams. Officials said that the damage was done at night under cover of darkness, but any team found to be placing muti would be banned from the field.

Muti and other magical interventions are common in African soccer. In many countries, teams have sorcerers or "juju men" who accompany the team to games to work charms and potions. "Departing for an international competition without consulting or including sorcerers is akin to going to an exam without a pencil," the editors of *African Soccer* magazine wrote of the practice. In an effort not to appear superstitious, however, the league that governs the sport suggested that the magic workers be put on the payroll as "team advisors" instead.

When working on the new Yankee Stadium in New York, a Boston Red Sox fan who was working construction on the site decided to have some fun and bury a Red Sox shirt under the field. Yankees management paid $50,000 to have it unearthed and threatened the prankster with legal action. After it was exhumed, the David Ortiz jersey was donated to the Jimmy Fund, the official Red Sox charity, which works with cancer patients. It was then auctioned on eBay for a final bid of $175,000. Yankee officials said that the auction proved that what was intended to be a curse actually turned into a blessing for cancer patients who will benefit from the sale.

Patron Saint of Real Estate

An old superstition from European Catholic countries took on a new meaning during the real estate downturn that started in the US in 2007. Burying a statue of St. Joseph upside down in the backyard is said to help home sellers find a buyer. The practice supposedly dates back to medieval times, when a convent wanted to buy a piece of property. St. Joseph is the patron saint of homes, so the nuns buried his statue in the land and they were able to purchase it. While the practice was once only known to Catholics, the real estate crisis encouraged others to give it a try. "St. Joseph Home Selling Kits" are available at hardware stores and online retailers.

Clover-rated

Four-leaf clovers are universally regarded as good luck charms. Each leaf is said to bring a different virtue: faith, hope, luck, and love (but the luck only kicks in if the clover is found by accident). In medieval Europe, clovers were thought to facilitate communication with fairies. The odds of finding a four-leaf clover are 10,000 to one. Despite their rarity, an Alaska man claims to have a collection of four-leaf clovers numbering over 160,000. An English boy in Wiltshire found a seven-leaf clover in 2009, but his find didn't quite come close to the 18-leaf clover found by a Japanese man in 2000. The same man bred a 56-leaf clover, but since he didn't come upon it by accident, it's not considered to hold any power.

Less than Charming Charms

Certain ethnic groups in South Africa believe that a vulture's eyesight is so good that the creepy bird can see into the future. With such great vision, it's bound to be able to see what number will win the lottery tomorrow, right? That's the reasoning behind the superstition of bringing a vulture's head along as a muti or lucky charm when picking lottery numbers. The belief has actually led poachers to lure vultures to poisoned animal carcasses that the vulture will then eat, causing them to die. Vultures are already a threatened species in the area and killing them is illegal according to traditional Zulu law. But since some will pay up to $1,000 for a vulture head muti, the poachers are really the ones who get lucky when they find a willing buyer (as long as they don't get caught).

In the hoodoo (folk magic) tradition of the American South, a raccoon penis bone (scientifically known as the *baculum*) is a lucky charm used to attract love. In some areas, it's boiled to remove any trace of the animal, and then tied to a red ribbon and worn as a necklace. In other areas, the bones were traditionally given to girls and young women by suitors, and in still other places, the charms are worn by men. Earrings made from cast raccoon penis bones became a fad in 2004, and celebrities such as Sarah Jessica Parker and Vanessa Williams were photographed wearing them. New Orleans gamblers are said to use the bones (also called coon dogs and Texas toothpicks) for luck.

While vulture heads and raccoon bacula may strike some as strange and unsavory, most don't even blink at a severed rabbit's foot. The luck-bringing fetish isn't as popular today as it was in the 1950s, but it's one of the most recognized charms in the world. The lucky rabbit's foot has mysterious origins—some trace it to the ancient Celts and Anglo Saxons, while others say it's an African tradition brought to the US by enslaved people.

Historians speculate that the rabbit was thought to be lucky either because of its remarkable fertility or for its burrowing habit, which would have put it in closer contact to the underworld. Whatever the origin, it became associated with hoodoo in the US by the 20th century and experienced a surge of popularity in the 1950s when vendors started selling the charm as key chains. Today, synthetic rabbit's feet are available for the squeamish.

Even the most diehard luck seekers would probably hesitate to carry one of the oldest good luck charms in the world: the

Who says they're good luck!?

swastika. Before it was co-opted as a symbol of the Nazis, it was known for its positive connotations in cultures from ancient Greece to Central America. In English-speaking cultures, it was said to bring the four L's represented in its sides: life, luck, light, and love. In the early days of aviation, pilots often wore swastika charms for good luck, and turn-of-the 20th-century sports teams often used it as their logo. While in the West, the image has been tarnished because of its association with the Nazis, it's still a common spiritual symbol in Asia.

Jinxed Jewels

If superstitions are to be believed, the Hope Diamond—said to be one of the largest and most perfect blue diamonds in the world—holds bad luck for any who possess it. The diamond is thought to be the same one that was earlier called The French Blue, which was purchased in India in the mid 1600s by a French merchant (although later stories—fabri-

Oh, honey, you shouldn't have. Really. You shouldn't have.

cated to enhance the gem's mystique—say that it was one of a matching pair that made up the eyes of a goddess). Tales of the "curse" didn't start until 1909, and none of them could be substantiated. The diamond is now in the Smithsonian

Museum in Washington, DC.

The Delhi Purple Sapphire (which is actually an amethyst) has a more ominous story. According to legend, it was looted by a British soldier from the Temple of Indra in Cawnpore (now Kanpur) during the Indian Mutiny of 1857. The soldier later lost all his money, and his son, who inherited the stone, suffered the same fate. A Victorian scientist who came to possess it gave it away to two friends who asked for it. One—a singer—lost her voice and never sang again. The other committed suicide. The scientist owner put it inside seven boxes surrounded by protective charms and a note that said: "This stone is trebly (sic) accursed and stained with the blood and dishonor of everyone who has ever owned it. Whoever shall open it shall read this warning first and then do as he pleases with the jewel. My advice to him or her is to cast it into the sea." He then donated it to the Natural History Museum in London with instructions that it not be touched till after his death. A curator who brought the gemstone to a symposium says that on the way back from the meeting, he was caught in the most terrifying thunderstorm he had ever experienced, and later developed a violent stomach bug and kidney stones. The trebly accursed gem is now on display at the museum.

Charmed Hollywood

Director Stephen Spielberg is said to keep an E.T. charm in the glove compartment of his car. Actress Cameron Diaz always wears a necklace given to her by a friend in order to stave off aging. Patrick Dempsey wears a pair of lucky shoes when he indulges in his sideline occupation—racecar driving. On the other hand, actor Christian Bale—who has a bit of a bad boy reputation—says he walks under ladders intentionally to provoke superstitions. Cate Blanchett keeps the elf ears she wore for her role in *The Lord of the Rings* trilogy on her mantel for good luck.

Charmed Politics

President McKinley always wore a red carnation in his buttonhole for good luck. It's said that on the day of his assassination, he gave it to a little girl in the crowd. Just minutes later, he was shot.

SOMETHING WICKED

For every superstition about luck or good fortune, there seems to be ten about the forces of evil. One thing is certain: True believers never let rationality get in the way of a good story or a superstitious explanation for things.

Are You a Good Witch or a Bad Witch?

Superstitions about witches may seem like a thing of the past, but they're very much still part of many cultures around the world. In several African countries, such superstitions have become even more prevalent in recent years as economic forces and poor heath lead people to seek reasons to explain forces outside of their control. Witch hysteria has gripped several countries, causing people to go after women—especially older widows—and attacking or even killing them. In 2007, three women and a man were beheaded in a rural Indian village after they were accused of sorcery. In 2009, a whole village in rural India was deserted when ten people came down with a mysterious illness, and it was assumed to be the work of a witch.

Belief in witches and witchcraft is so widespread in Tanzania that the government recently launched a newspaper called *The Big Pot* to combat the superstition. One of the goals of the paper is to make people aware that they are being cheated by witch doctors who sell "cures" that can reverse the spells of witches.

Not all modern witches are considered to be evil, though. In the UK, a football (soccer) team with an unbroken streak of losses on its home field hired a "white witch" or good witch, to help improve their luck. The local witch, who has written eleven books on witchcraft, performed a series of rituals to lift the curse on the team's home ground. The band Fall Out Boy hired a witch doctor to lift a curse on its US tour, which had been dogged by technical difficulties, food poisoning, and injuries to road crew.

In 2008, in the Democratic Republic of Congo, rumors of penis snatchings and shrinkings by sorcerers spread across the capital, causing panic and inciting mobs. A radio program warned listeners that sorcerers were afoot that could make one's penis shrink or disappear with the touch of a hand. In particular, men wearing gold rings and riding in the local bush taxis (an inexpensive, informal, van-sized form of transportation) were said to be suspect. Police took thirteen men into protective custody when there were several attempted lynchings, and also arrested alleged victims of the sorcerers—men that they said were trying to extort money out of the superstitious by offering a cure for the horrible curse. The incident followed a similar one that happened in Ghana in the previous decade. Twelve alleged penis-snatchers were beaten to death by angry mobs.

In Romania, witchcraft is considered a profession, and it's not unusual for witches to operate storefronts offering potions and fortune-telling. In recent years, Romanian witches have developed an online presence in order to get a leg up on the competition and reach customers in other parts of the world. Their more modern services include gay love potions and charms that improve the chances of winning European Union grant money.

The Voodoo That You Do

Voodoo is recognized by the governments of Benin and Haiti as an official religion and is considered by anthropologists to be a legitimate belief system. There are over four million believers in Benin, which now celebrates a Voodoo Day national holiday. In Haiti, close to 100% of the population practices voodoo, regardless of their other religious affiliations. There are still some people, however, who practice what voodoo believers call black magic, under the name of voodoo.

A South Carolina woman claiming to be a voodoo priestess reported that a Georgia county commissioner approached her about putting a hex on her opponent prior to an upcoming election. The self-proclaimed priestess said that the check the official had written to her bounced, so she never actually performed the hex rite, but she did sacrifice a chicken and three roosters for the commissioner at no charge. The commissioner was later roundly defeated in the election.

In the UK, a woman who was charged with defrauding the

government for nearly £1 million said that the reason she had used fake social security numbers and invented families to collect tax credits and benefits was because she was under a voodoo curse. The woman also claimed that the curse had also caused her daughter to lose three fingers and pulled severed digits out of her purse at the trial as "proof." She was convicted of fraud and jailed. The actual source of the fingers is under investigation.

The Devil's in the Fuse Box

Sicily is known as one of the more superstitious parts of Italy. When residents in nine different homes in a small costal town there experienced a series of unexplained electrical fires, flare-ups, and other incidents, people became convinced that it was the work of the devil.

A television in one home exploded and fuse boxes in several houses on one street went out. Appliances started to smoke, including an air conditioner that wasn't plugged in.

Electric car door locks clicked up and down by themselves, cell phones rang even though no one was on the line, and a large fire broke out, forcing people from their homes. Some scientists said the fires were the result of supercharged ions created by volcanic activity in the area, while others said that there was no obvious explanation. Italy's electrical service provider cut power to the city and rewired it, ending the incidents. Residents said that if it happened again, they would have to make a sacrifice to the gods, such as a black goat or black sheep, and bury it in the ground, according to an ancient superstition about exorcising demons.

The Mummy's Curse

Ever since 18th-century Egyptologists started opening the tombs of ancient pharaohs, tales of curses have persisted. According to the superstitions, the high priests of Egypt sealed the tombs with curses dooming whoever dared disturb the king's passage into the afterlife. Some said that the curses

Don't worry, not all of you will die.

were even engraved on the doors of the tombs, and actually spelled out how intruders would meet their end.

The most famous of the superstitions is known as King Tut's

Curse. When the pharaoh's tomb was opened in 1922, several of those who worked on the excavation suffered unexplained seizures and died within years of the tomb's discovery. Lord Carnarvon, the British archeologist who financed the dig, died just a few weeks after the tomb was opened. Although the press has cited twenty-one as the number of those who died after working on the tomb, the number was closer to half a dozen. Scientists have speculated that the tombs actually contained toxins that may have contributed to the illnesses and deaths. However, many of those who worked on the dig lived into their eighties.

A German man who stole an artifact from the Valley of the Kings in 2007 was struck with inexplicable fever, paralysis, and then death upon his return to his home country, according to a living relative. The relative, who made sure the artifact got back to Egypt, feared the man had been victim to a curse.

King Tut isn't the only one whose tomb is said to be cursed. It's believed that William Shakespeare himself wrote the curse that can be found above his grave in Holy Trinity Church in Stratford-Upon-Avon: "Blest be the man that spares these stones, And curst be he that moves my bones." The curse was taken seriously when church officials undertook the task of restoring the Bard's badly deteriorating tomb. Restorers were instructed not to touch the bones inside the coffin.

The Iceman Cometh

A mummy of a different sort—the Iceman—soon became the subject of curse rumors after he was unearthed in the Swiss Alps. Dubbed "Otzi" by scientists, the 3000-plus-year-old man had been preserved in a glacier until a hiker discovered him in melting ice in 1991. Within a decade, seven people associated with Otzi research had died. The hiker who had discovered him fell to his death in a blizzard. The head of the rescue team trying to find him had a heart attack. The mountaineer who had led a forensics expert to the mummy died in an avalanche, and the expert died in a car crash on his way to give a lecture about the Iceman. The journalist who filmed the Iceman's removal from the ice died of a brain tumor, and an archeologist who wrote a book about the Iceman died of an inherited blood disease before the book could be released. If the Iceman cometh, perhaps it's best to runneth.

Curse of the Ninth

A little-known curse, the Curse of the Ninth dictates that a composer who has completed his ninth symphony will soon die. The best-known victims of the curse are Beethoven and Mahler. (Mahler started a tenth symphony, but died before it was completed.) There are eight other composers who are thought to be fatalities of the curse, including Franz Schubert, Anton Bruckner, and Antonin Dvorak. However, this is one superstition that has fallen suspect due to a lot of fuzzy math.

School's Out

In the Philippines in 2009, a high school in Sarangani province had to cancel classes indefinitely because, officials said, eighty students had been possessed by evil spirits. School administrators believed the school had been haunted for some time, but after a religious group arrived to pray at the school, the spirits started to take possession of students, causing them to collapse in epileptic-like fits in the hallways. Some students claimed that they were being haunted by five angry dwarves. Officials decided to close the school while working with church leaders to find a solution for ridding the school of demons.

Island of Vampires

The island of Santorini is now one of Greece's top tourist attractions, but it was once known as "The Island of the Vampires." In Greece, a corpse was suspected of being a vampire if the body didn't decompose on schedule. It's now believed that volcanic ash in Santorini's soil helped preserve bodies, but in the past, Santorini was seen as a vampire haven. Suspected vampire corpses from other parts of Greece were even sent to Santorini for containment because it was thought that vampires couldn't cross water.

In Italy, suspected vampires were buried with a brick wedged between their jaws to keep them from eating through their funeral shroud and eating the flesh of other corpses in the graveyard. In 2008, archeologists found the skeleton of one of these "vampires" near Venice, the brick still in place in her mouth.

The Curse of Good Luck

Many dream of winning the lottery, but some of those who actually have won said its more a curse than a blessing. A pair of friends in England who won on a ticket purchased together, both later divorced and their friendship ended. A

Ihth cahm hoo uuch uur bhlood!

Congratulations Mr. Miller, you've just won our . . .
hey, do you smell smoke?

couple who won ended their marriage just months later. A man who won £2 million died less than two years later, after retreating to his home and descending into alcoholism. One lottery winner was kidnapped and murdered by his sister-in-law. The man who won the biggest individual lottery payout in US history (over $300 million) became more famous for his bad luck than his winnings. He was hounded for money everywhere he went. His business was sued, his wife left him, and he was robbed. His granddaughter became a drug addict and was later found dead.

BODYGUARDS

Garlic necklaces, silver bullets, mirrors, and crosses—they're all in the toolkit of the superstition person wanting to ward off evil. While you may have heard of some of these body-guards, some of these lesser known ways of protecting your-self and your home from the forces of evil may take you by surprise.

If These Walls Could Talk

In 2008, while renovating the historic lieutenant governor's residence in Halifax, Nova Scotia, a construction crew found eight women's shoes built into the plaster and lathe walls of the early 19th-century home. Researching the odd find, the project manager discovered that the crew had stumbled upon "concealment shoes," part of an evil-evading custom that peaked in popularity in Great Britain and North America during the time the residence was built.

According to an old English superstition, evil spirits can enter a home through its walls. Starting around the 1400s, people put dead human bodies under new homes to scare off demons. When that practice proved too smelly, they turned to shoes. The shoe, it was believed, was the garment that most closely resembled an actual part of the human anatomy. (A dress or shirt was thought to be too shapeless.) There's also speculation that an evil spirit could become trapped in a shoe, thus unable to enter the home.

While constructing a new house, shoes would be placed into the walls near openings such as doors, windows, or fireplaces. Superstitious homebuilders typically used worn out women's or children's shoes, always in singles, never in pairs. Keeping away evil was important, but most people were too poor to waste a perfectly good pair of shoes to do it. According to English historians, immigrants from the British Isles brought the practice to North America, and people renovating historic homes along the Eastern seaboard often find them during the process.

The crew at the Halifax home decided to keep the tradition alive and wrapped eight separate modern-day shoes in plastic bags along with notes explaining the story before stuffing them back into the walls throughout the house. The original shoes went to Government House in Halifax to be put on display. The Northampton Museum in Northampton England has more than 2,000 concealment shoes in its collection.

Safe as Houses

In Scandinavian countries, an acorn is placed on a window-sill to prevent lightning from striking the house. The custom comes from a Norse myth about Thor, the god of thunder, who was said to have been saved from lightning by taking shelter under an oak tree. Acorns are often used as a motif in curtain pulls and window hardware as a result of this su-perstition.

In Himalayan cultures, some people ward off evil spirits by spreading a layer of cow dung on the floor or burying a horse skull under the house. Some also set traps outside the house to keep the demons from getting in.

In Bhutan, an image of a penis is said to ward off evil. People

Crap!

in rural areas paint penises on the outside of their homes in order to protect those in the house from the evil eye and ensure harmony within the home. In the monastery where the superstition is said to have started, people can go to be blessed by being hit on the head with a wooden phallus. This ritual is also said to improve fertility for women.

Boomerang Effect

Can evil spirits be bounced from one home to the next with the aid of mirrors? In one Chinese city, residents in neighboring high rises seem to think so. Sensing that evil was emanating from a neighbor's home and drifting towards their own, a family hung six mirrors on top of a red cloth on their balcony in an effort to deflect the evil streaming toward their home in the direction of another neighbor's apartment. That neighbor responded by hanging two mirrors and a pair of red underwear, in an effort to redirect the evil back to its original location. No one in the axis of evil would remove

Whatever bounces off me, sticks to you!

the deflectors unless the others did so first.

Heads Up

In 2006, a woman was arrested after arriving at Miami's air-

We need to head this one off!

port with a human head in her suitcase. The woman, who was arriving from Haiti, was a believer in voodoo and said that the head was intended to ward off evil spirits. She was charged with failing to declare the head.

A voodoo priest in Ghana was accused of robbing his own grandmother's grave to use her head for a customer needing protection.

The Evil Eye

Belief in the evil eye—an evil force evoked when one person envies another—is rampant in many areas of the world, having originated, scholars think, in the Middle East and Mediterranean and spread as far as India. The evil eye brings all kinds of misfortune, from ruined crops to illness, to car accidents to death, all through "looking at" a person and praising him or her. In many cultures, giving the evil eye is not necessarily an intentional thing—the evil eye can work through an unsuspecting person to bring misfortune to another. A Saudi Arabian man, for example, got a compliment on his Porsche. Although his mother had put seeds in the car to protect him from the evil eye, they had been vacuumed up when he had the car cleaned. When he crashed the car, all familiar with the situation were sure the accident was due to the evil eye.

In many countries, from the Mediterranean all he way to Ireland, if you inadvertently compliment someone (thus attracting the attention of the evil eye), you can counteract your statement by then spitting at the person.

In Greece, the beautiful bright blue roofs seen on white-washed houses aren't just there for aesthetic purposes—blue is said to ward of the evil eye. Blue beads are hung over door-ways—the glass is said to reflect the evil eye back onto itself. Eyes are also painted on walls in blue paint. Greek jewelry often features eye-shaped charms and blue glass beads worn on the wrists or around the neck. In Middle Eastern countries, blue beads are sometimes wound around the front grille of cars and buses, attached to horse harnesses, and pinned to children's clothes. A potted cactus near the door is also supposed to keep the evil eye off a Greek home.

In Italy, the evil eye is called *malocchio*. To keep it away one wears a *cornuto* (devil's horn) or a *mano fico* (fig hand) amulet, each of which features a hand making a different rude gesture.

A survivor of a China air crash in Japan credited his survival with the nine-eyed amulet he was holding in his hand at the time.

In India, a string is run through a lemon and a chili pepper, and then tied at one end and wrapped around a nail over a home's door in order to keep the evil eye away.

In India, evil eye amulets called *drishti kaya* are commonly sold from carts in the streets. The amulets are hung over the threshold of a home to keep out the evil eye.

A Ukrainian immigrant to the US started a new line of clothing purported to deflect the evil eye. Called Lucky Stella, the product line includes hats and shirts featuring the "lucky eye," which, of course, is an antidote to the evil eye. The product line became instantly popular after music and movie celebrities and their children were seen wearing items from it.

Wild Things

WE all know that we can't control nature, and in fact, many times *it* controls *us*. There are however, some things we can do to appease it or to at least avoid incurring its wrath: avoid taking rocks from Hawaiian beaches for example, lest the volcano goddess invoke a curse, and avoid cutting trees that may be home to fairies or other little people. On the other hand, we are all powerless to the almighty robin: If one flies into your house, you're done for.

FUR, FANGS, FEATHERS, AND FINS

From the humble pig to the elusive dolphin, animals are thought to have the power to bring you luck or bring you down.

The Black Cat

When a black cat crosses your path, you'll have bad luck: it's one of the best known superstitions in the world. In medieval

Um . . . honey . . . better put that down.

Europe, black cats were associated with the devil because the light in their eyes was said to be proof of demonic possession. They gained a reputation as witches' familiars, tasked with going out and doing evil for witches. Some believed that witches could actually shape shift into black cats. Pope Innocent VIII even decreed that owning a cat was punishable by death, and millions of cats were killed in and around Europe.

While fear of black cats may sound positively medieval, there's a lot of proof the superstition is still thriving in the 21st century. In 2003, neighbors in an Israeli apartment building joined together to file a complaint about a fellow resident's black cat. Running into it in the stairwell would get their day off to a bad start, they said. The group entreated a local veterinarian to support their claim that running into a black cat—especially in the dark—was an unfair imposition on neighbors, and that the cat be held in the arms of its owner while in public areas of the building. The cat's owner said that the cat was being singled out because of its color.

In Milan, Italy, a famous footballer was accused of killing a black cat that frequented the team's training facility because he blamed the cat for the team's string of bad luck. The player denied it. The killing of black cats remains frequent in Italy though, so much so that an animal rights group declared Black Cat Day to raise awareness about abuse of black cats.

It is said that Winston Churchill, who had several cats, believed that petting a black cat would counteract bad luck. His black cat Nelson was reputed to have a chair at cabinet meetings.

What's Bugging You?

Insects are the subject of myriad superstitions. In ancient Egypt, scarab beetles were considered to be magical insects. Their habit of pushing dung balls called to mind the way the sun moved across the sky, so the beetle came to be associated with the sun god (and also with resurrection because of the way the sun came back after setting each day). Scarab beetle amulets were often put over the hearts of mummies to protect them for their journey into the afterlife.

Spiders are thought to be good luck in most cultures. In Native American myth, the world is said to have been created by a giant spider woman who spun it into existence. Spiders are also thought to be "grandmothers" or female ancestors who bring messages to the living, so harming them would be like hurting a respected elder.

In Islamic countries, spiders are considered lucky because there's a story about a spider protecting the prophet Mohammed when he was hiding from an enemy inside a cave. The spider covered the entire entrance to the cave with a web, so the enemy did not enter. In Christianity, there is an almost identical story about a spider spinning a web over a cave where Mary and Joseph were hiding from King Herod's men who wanted to kill the baby Jesus.

Spiders' spinning ability spurred an association with money, and in some cultures they are called the "money spinners."

In Japan, seeing a spider in the morning is good luck, but bad luck at night. The opposite is true in France, where there is an old saying about the matter: "A spider seen in the morning is a sign of grief; a spider seen at noon, of joy; a spider seen in the evening, of hope."

A cricket in the home (or on the hearth) is a sign of good luck in most European countries. In China, crickets are a very important symbol of luck. Raising crickets is a common hobby in China, and crickets are sold in pots, tubes, or wooden cages in just about every marketplace. In Shanghai, there are twenty markets devoted exclusively to crickets. Crickets are generally divided into two categories: singing and fighting. While an ordinary singing cricket sells for around 12¢, a fighting cricket (which is put in a cage with another to see which prevails) sometimes goes for thousands of dollars.

Magpie Magic

In Native American culture, the magpie is considered to be a magical bird, and indeed a shaman in disguise. In China and Korea, its chattering is said to herald the arrival of guests or other good news.

In England, the magpie's effect depends on the number of birds seen: "One for sorrow, two for joy, three for girl, four for boy, five for silver, six for gold, seven for a secret never to be told." In some parts of England, if you do see a single magpie, you can counteract its bad luck by doffing your cap in its direction. In other areas, you should speak to the bird, saying, "Good morning, Mr. Magpie. How is your lady wife today?" This kills two birds with one stone, so to speak, by showing the magpie respect and thus decreasing the chances that he'll bring you bad luck, while at the same time, implying that there are two magpies, which equals joy.

In Scotland, the magpie is said to carry a drop of the devil's blood on its tongue, and if the bird is a seen through the window of a house, death will soon follow. In Yorkshire, England, one should make the sign of the cross when seeing a magpie.

In the Isle of Man off the coast of England, wrens were said to be the bad-luck birds, and at Christmas time they were hunted, and then brought to a church where they were buried while people sang and danced around a decorated wooden pole.

As the Crow Flies

While the crow portends death in many European cultures, in India, crows can bring good luck if you happen to find one that's entrapped and free it. In Hyderabad, you can buy a crow specifically for the purpose of setting it free and bringing yourself good luck. For the small fee of 50 rupees, it's possible to open the crow's cage and release it. Along with the crow's release, will come a release from any type of conflict that one is currently experiencing, such as marital or financial problems. City officials say, however, that the caging actually weakens the bird's ability to fly, and that soon after their release, they are often recaptured and sold again.

Fishy Stuff

Dolphins were considered sacred to the ancient Greeks, and in many seafaring cultures it is said that they arrived at the sides of ships during storms so that they could carry the sailors to safety should the vessel be destroyed. For this reason, they started to be associated with bad weather at sea. Dolphins are also said to have healing powers. There are numerous "dolphin therapy" programs in Europe and North

131

and South America, aimed at healing those with depression or mental illness. Animal rights activists say these programs don't really help humans and are unlucky for dolphins, who should be set free.

In China, fish are associated with wealth and good luck. The *arowana* or dragonfish is particularly lucky because it's thought to be a descendent of the magical dragon, which is the luckiest of creatures. Dragonfish, which can live up to twenty-five years, sell for anywhere between $2,000 and $10,000 in China.

When a Golden Cash Tiger Fish (whose scales resemble gold coins) was caught off the coast of Zhanjiang, a restaurant paid $75,000 for it. Meals made from the fish were sold at a loss, but the restaurant owners believed that the good luck brought by the fish would eventually bring them more money.

This Little Piggy

Pigs are considered good luck in Germany. The *glucksschwien* or good luck pig is found in charms, toys, and candy, which are given away on Christmas and New Year's. When something fortunate happens, people will say the recipient of the luck has "had pig." Before the 2006 Winter Olympics, an Austrian skier was given a real pig for good luck. She won a silver medal in the women's slalom event.

Snakes on the Brain

In India, certain types of snakes are considered to be reincarnated gods, so it's taboo to harm or provoke them. Since peacocks have been thought to have power over snakes, it's believed that holding a peacock feather over a snake bite will cure it. Health officials say more than 50,000 people a year die in India from snake bites because victims go to witch doctors or try superstitious cures instead of seeking medical attention.

Here, use this!

Going back to ancient Greece, snakes were thought to hold a glowing stone inside their bodies that could be used for healing. Accounts from her time say that Queen Victoria had one that had been handed down to her from Queen

Elizabeth I, who was known to be able to cure people with the touch of her hand. (Some speculated her power came from holding the snake stone hidden in her palm.)

In Japan, snakes—especially white ones—are associated with good fortune. Snakeskin wallets are popular because they're thought to attract money. Among the Luo people of Kenya, the appearance of a python bodes well, as long as it's treated well. Some of those in the group have converted to Christianity though, and they have become to see this traditional good omen as a bad one. Clashes have arisen over whether to protect the snake or kill it.

MAGICAL THINKING

In the stage version of the classic tale *Peter Pan*, audiences are asked to clap if they believe in fairies, because it's only this belief that will keep the tiny winged creatures alive. If that's the case, fairies don't have much to worry about. Belief in them still runs strong in northern Europe. In fact, the fair folk even have a say in what gets built where.

Fairy Tales

In Ireland, there were thought to be myriad different types of fairies. While some fairies were considered benevolent good folk, many were tricksters with evil intent, who would steal human children and replace them with fairy changelings. Because fairies dislike mistletoe, families in Ireland and Scotland would place a sprig of mistletoe over a baby's cradle to thwart fairies in their baby-stealing attempts. This is the origin of the Christmas mistletoe tradition: Kissing under the bow ensured protection for the couple in a place where fairies couldn't sabotage their love.

The pooka fairy was a shape-shifter, often appearing in animal form, but always with yellow eyes. In some areas, he was said to come at night, destroying crops and breaking fences so that livestock could run free. In others, he was more of a playful trickster. Variations of the pooka exist in Cornwall and Devon, England; Wales; and Scotland. In the 1950 Jimmy Stewart movie *Harvey,* the 6-foot-tall bunny—visible only to Stewart's character—was said by the screenwriter to be a film version of a pooka.

Fairies were said to gather at night in fairy rings—areas where mushrooms grow in a circle or semicircle. While rare, they're a natural occurrence that happens when mushrooms spread their spores in a circular pattern. In some areas of England, they were said to be caused by fairies wearing down the grass with their dancing, while in others, the rings were chalked up to fairies riding their horses in a circle. In Denmark, the circles are attributed to elf parties, while in Austria it's said that the grass is scorched by dragon's breath. In some areas, the custom is to make a wish on a fairy ring. In others, it's necessary to avoid the area, lest the fairies retaliate for ruining their party grounds. In most places, it's considered very bad luck to trample on a fairy's mushroom.

The Three Wishes Faery Festival happens each year in Cornwall, the part of Britain most strongly associated with fairies. In Cornwall, the "small people" include *piskeys*, mischievous magical creatures, and *spriggan*, tiny people who are quite malicious. When building a house in the area, it was common to leave a hole to allow the small people to come in and out.

A group in Washington State holds a Fairy and Human Relations Congress each year to increase awareness of "the subtle realms" and the beings who inhabit them. Participants attend workshops to help them learn to tune in to fairy energy and improve communication between the worlds.

In Saudi Arabia, belief in genies still runs strong. One Saudi family who claimed to be plagued by a menacing genie even went so far as to take the spirit to court. The genie had been harassing the family for over two years, they said, throwing rocks at them when they left their home, stealing their cell phones, and leaving them threatening voicemails. In order to protect themselves, they moved into a home provided by a local charity. It's not clear what legal recourse the family hoped to get from the suit, but court officials said that the complaint was to be taken seriously and that an investigation was underway.

The Fairy Bridge

On the Isle of Man, between England and Ireland, locals and visitors alike regularly stop to pay their respects to the fairies at the Fairy Bridge. Those who cross but fail to say hello will receive bad luck, the superstition says. The practice dates back as far as anyone can remember, though some historians say that it can be traced to the 12th century, when the bridge

I don't believe this fairy rubbish.

formed the boundary to an old abbey. Saying hello to the fairies, they say, replaced the old custom of making the sign of the cross at the bridge. Before the annual motorcycle rally held on the island, riders go to the bridge to greet the fairies, lest they end up in a roadway collision.

As New Age beliefs gained popularity in the 1980s and beyond, people began to leave notes and wishes tied to the bridge. The practice later extended to tying extraneous items such as fuzzy dice or bras to the bridge, proving a "distraction to motorists" local officials said. A shop owner came up with the idea for a "fairy post box" where the items and letters could be contained.

Blame the Pixies

In the Czech Republic, mischievous house sprites are often blamed for small household accidents such as things falling and breaking. If the number of incidents increases, the sprites can be appeased by leaving a bowl of milk out for them. In many European cultures, house pixies are said to turn milk sour, while others hide or steal household items and jewelry. In Turkey, it's inadvisable to go swimming in a lake at dusk or at night because the jinn (genie) or pixies will steal your soul while you're in the water.

Fairy's Right of Way

In Iceland, belief in the *huldufolk*, or hidden people, is widespread. Building projects must be cleared with them before getting underway. Permission is granted via an elf communicator who can find out if the beings are present. If they are and are not consulted, the little people will make their disapproval known by causing glitches in machinery or creating other unexpected difficulties.

In the 1970s, a road construction project was altered because elves were believed to live in nearby rocks. Later, construction on an aluminum plant was delayed for six months for verification that no elves or hidden people would be displaced by the project.

In many areas of Ireland, it's believed that a single hawthorn tree situated in a field is a fairy meeting place. One particular hawthorn in County Clare, known as the "Fairy Tree of Latoon," became known as the place where the local fairies would stop when returning from their wars with fairies in neighboring Connacht. Farmers reported finding greenish fairy blood near the tree, speculating that the fairies had dragged their wounded to the tree to be treated. Harming the tree was considered very inadvisable. A local storyteller led a group in a successful fight to divert a planned motorway from the path of the tree and erect a fence around it for protection. The tree had become a popular tourist attraction until someone cut it down with a chainsaw under cover of darkness. County Clare's football team lost a match the very same week. But just weeks later, leaves started to sprout from the stump, proving to some that the fairies would not be deterred.

FORCES OF NATURE

Nature can be a bit unpredictable: violent storms, earth-quakes, volcanoes—it's no wonder humans have made up a slew of superstitions to help make sense of the sometimes random, sometimes benevolent elements that Mother Nature sends our way.

Thunder and Lightning

In Japan, when children hear thunder, they are instructed to hide their bellybuttons or the thunder god Raijin will try to eat them. In many cultures, swans are associated with the thunder gods.

In ancient India and Greece, it was believed that swans would only hatch when thunder clapped or lightning struck their shell. A swan craning its neck was said to portend a thunderstorm. Beware strong winds if you see a swan take flight.

In Europe, churches used to ring their bells during thunderstorms to send out protection over the town. In England, people used to grow house leeks (a kind of wild onion) on their thatched roofs to ward off lightning. The conqueror Charlemagne even ordered that all roofs in the domain should have them. The English also used to wear a bay leaf or a laurel leaf under their clothes to protect against lightning strikes. Thunderstorms were also thought to turn beer sour unless a cold iron bar was placed in the barrel.

In Bali, Indonesia, superstition dictates that you should throw a knife in the yard during a storm so that the lightning will strike the object instead of a person. This belief also exists in Turkey. In Cambodia, it's believed that people with moles on their calves and people who have broken promises are more likely to get struck by lightning.

Moonlight Madness and Other Moon Myths

It's a long-held superstition in many cultures that the full moon causes a spike in crime, a higher than normal number of births, and an increase in the number of people doing crazy things. While anecdotal evidence from emergency-room nurses and police officers implies otherwise, sociologists say that "moonlight madness" is just a superstition. Historians speculate that the perception that people do crazy things when the moon is full stems from the fact that before electricity was invented, people generally stayed indoors while it was dark out. When the moon was full, more people were outdoors and, as a consequence, were liable to commit crimes or otherwise engage in activities they wouldn't normally pursue. As for the full-moon baby speculations, they spring from the ancient association of the moon with fertility. But repeated scientific studies show no correlation between moon phases and the number of births. In Turkey, it's believed that babies born under a full moon will "shine" in life, and girls will be especially beautiful.

There may, however, be some truth to the old farmer's belief that the full moon is the best time for planting. After the new moon and before the full moon, the earth's gravitation pull is reduced, so it's easier for plants to stretch away from the earth, up and out. After the full moon, the moon's gravitation pull is reduced, so it's easier for roots to dig down deeper. There's also a very slight electrical charge in plants that increases when lunar pull is increased, so that helps them grow, too.

Shadows Over the Sun

In ancient China and Thailand, an eclipse was thought to be a dragon trying to eat the sun. People would shoot off firecrackers to try to scare it away.

When an eclipse was predicted just a week before the 2008

Summer Olympics in Beijing, authorities tried to quell anxieties about the games by publicizing assurances from feng shui experts that the solar event could be safely ignored since it would bring minor disturbances in the market and nothing more.

In India, an eclipse is said by to be caused by the angry god Rahu, who is trying to eat the sun. People bang pots and pans during an eclipse to try to frighten him off. It's believed in India that if a pregnant woman goes outside during an eclipse, her baby will be born disfigured or blind. Food left out during an eclipse is said to be rendered impure and should be thrown out. When the longest (three minutes) solar eclipse in modern times took place in July 2009, some Indian astrologers predicted that a major political leader would be killed or there would be a significant attack by Kashmiri separatists during or immediately following the eclipse. Other astrologers saw a natural disaster—such as a tsunami or earthquake—as the result. Indian hospitals saw a spike in the number of requests for scheduled C-sections from pregnant women desperate to make sure their baby was not born during the eclipse. In China, where the eclipse was also visible, astrologers predicted that the possibility of war in the aftermath of the eclipse was 95%. The eclipse passed without tumultuous events.

Tunnel Vision

In Japan, there's an old superstition that if a woman enters a tunnel that's under construction, the mountain goddess, who is jealous of other women, will become angry and curse the construction workers. Women are prohibited by law from working on tunnel construction, and a female reporter was once barred from covering the ribbon-cutting at a tunnel because of the superstition. The first known case of a woman entering a tunnel that was not yet complete came in the 1990s, when a female construction inspector was allowed to complete her evaluation of a tunnel project. The company directors deemed it safe because she was not actually working on the project, but only inspecting it. Female engineers have recently protested the legal restrictions that keep them out of tunnels, and lawmakers are said to be considering revising it.

Make It Rain

In the eastern Indian state of Bihar, it is believed that the weather gods can be shamed into sending rain during a drought. During a recent rainless stretch, farmers in the state sent their unmarried daughters into the fields to plough. The daughters had all the proper tools, but no clothes on. This was done in the hopes that the gods would be so embarrassed they would let it pour. This belief is apparently long-held and widespread in area, and is said to produce reliable results. The young girls sing ancient hymns while they plow with the help of elderly women.

In many Native American groups, dancing has always been a way to solicit the gods for rain. A Southern California water district hired a group of Chumash tribe members to perform a traditional water ceremony (not a rain dance) at their annual water awareness meeting just as a gesture to show "reverence for water." Just days after the performance, a four-month long drought in the area was interrupted by a "freak rainstorm."

Lucky Star?

Shooting stars are seen differently in different cultures. In England, it's said that a shooting star is a soul coming down from heaven before it comes to rest in a new baby. In Chinese culture, it was long believed that there is a star in the sky for each soul on earth, so that when one falls, it means someone is going to die. In other cultures, wishing on any star in the sky or the first star seen in the early evening sky will result in a wish come true. Still other cultures believe that shooting star wishes are singled out to be especially lucky.

Revenge of the Volcano Goddess

If there's one superstition that locals and visitors to Hawaii are sure to know it's this: If you visit Big Island and Hawaii Volcanoes National Park, whatever you do, don't take a anything away with you. You'll incur the wrath of Pele, the volcano goddess. Those who take a chance often end up believers. Park officials say that each year they receive numerous packages (many addressed to Pele) from people around the world who took lava rocks, sand, or shells during a visit to the park. The unfortunate tourists return the object along with a note explaining the bad luck that came with it. Offenders often plead that the curse be lifted. In Hawaiian culture, everything in nature has power and a place that ensures harmony, and permission must be asked before changing the order of things. It's also illegal to remove anything from the park, and doing so can lead to hefty fines.

From the
Cradle to
the Grave

L IFE's milestones are fraught with superstitions. New baby? You've got more to worry about than sleepless nights and colic—you've got to protect your little bundle from the evil eye. Getting married? Don't walk down that aisle without something borrowed, something blue, and a sixpence in your shoe. And don't let your loved one pass on to the great beyond without a cell phone in her casket—she may need it to call you in case she's not really dead.

OH, BABY

Few events in life conjure up as many superstitious beliefs as the birth of a child. From how to conceive one and how to determine the baby's gender to how to ensure an easy labor, each step along the way is subject to myriad superstitions aimed at creating a happy outcome. Though stemming from a past where childbirth was a much more dangerous pursuit, many of these superstitions persist today.

155

A Boy or a Girl?

To make sure that they will have a boy, a newly married couple in China must roll over their bed on the night of their wedding. In Turkey, a boy should be placed in the lap of the bride if she is to conceive a boy.

In Japan, it's believed that if a pregnant woman's husband eats a lot of bananas, she will give birth to a girl, while in England "bananas for boys" is a well-known saying. In some European cultures, if the mother craves sweets, she will have a girl; salty foods, it's a boy. One superstition says if the mother carries the baby high, it's a girl; low, it's a boy.

In some parts of India, pregnant women are advised that carrying a piece of marble will ensure that she gives birth to a boy. This superstition has led to the desecration of marble monuments in old British cemeteries—people cut off chunks of the statues and headstones to give to women who are expecting or would like to be.

Scientific studies show that "mother's intuition" is more than just a superstition: 70% of mothers accurately "guess" which gender their baby will be before they find out. Also, a study of 700 women in England did in fact show a correlation between eating bananas and giving birth to a boy; however, there was no evidence that the sweet for girls and salty for boys superstition was true.

What to Do (and Not Do)
While You're Expecting

In the Philippines, if a woman eats too many bananas during her pregnancy, it's said that her child will be bald and not be able to grow hair. In Indonesia, eating spicy food is said to lead to a baby with curly hair, while in Spanish-speaking countries, it's supposed to make a baby's hair darker. In Europe, spicy food is said to give mothers heartburn, which, in

Hey, trade you my banana.
No thanks. Had enough of those already.

turn, is supposed to lead to dark hair for the baby.

In Indonesia, drinking coconut juice during the latter part of your pregnancy is said to ensure a beautiful baby. In India, drinking milk laced with saffron is said to make your baby's skin lighter.

In the Philippines, eating dark foods, such as blueberries is said to make your baby's complexion darker.

It's a Jewish superstition that no clothes should be bought for the baby until after he or she arrives—to have clothes with no baby is to tempt fate.

The forty-day mark after a baby is born is seen as a significant milestone in many cultures. In some places, it's said that a baby does not receive its soul until his fortieth day. In Russia, folks say that only the parents should see a baby in the first forty days. In Islamic cultures, a woman should not go far from her home for the first forty days after giving birth. Some superstitions state she should not wash her hair until the forty-first day after giving birth.

In Australian Aboriginal tradition, a new baby is "smoked." A fire is made from conkerberry wood, and water is dripped over it to make smoke. Fragrant leaves are dropped into the fire and water is sprayed over the baby. The baby is then held briefly over the fire. The ritual is said to ensure that the baby will be healthy in life.

In China, a baby was traditionally not given a name for the first month because of the strong chance that he or she might not survive. After a month, the baby is given a name at a "red egg and ginger" party, where red envelopes stuffed with money are handed out to friends and family along with eggs dyed red and oranges for luck.

In many cultures, especially in the South Pacific, Caribbean, and Africa, children are first given a fake name to fool the evil spirits. Only the parents or close family members will know the child's real name until he or she is older.

Hey kid, the world out there isn't all it's cracked up to be.

In German tradition, a baby was taken out after six weeks, and then family and neighbors would tap on his or her lips with a "talking egg" three times to ensure that he or she would learn to speak quickly.

In many cultures, it's said that a baby should not see its own reflection in a mirror for the first year. Some say that the baby will die if he or she does. In the Dominican Republic, it's said that a baby won't learn to talk if he or she sees his reflection before reaching the age of two.

In Russia, if a baby urinates on one of the parents, it's said that the parent will live to dance at the child's wedding.

In India, a pregnant woman should not look at an eclipse or her baby will have birthmarks. In Pakistan, if she touches a sharp object during an eclipse, her baby will be born with a cleft lip or be missing a digit or limb. In Indonesia, if a pregnant woman harms any living thing, it's said her baby will be born with a disability.

In the rural US South, it was believed that looking at a dead person would cause a pregnant woman's baby to die.

Luck or no luck, the kid certainly has good aim.

In Indonesia, a man shouldn't eat while lying down or his wife will have a difficult labor. It's also believed that opening the windows and doors of the house will lead to an easier labor.

The Blessed Event

An old English rhyme says that the day of the week on which you are born has everything to do with your personality:

> *Monday's child is fair of face.*
> *Tuesday's child is full of grace.*
> *Wednesday's child is full of woe.*
> *Thursday's child has far to go.*
> *Friday's child is loving and giving.*
> *Saturday's child works hard for a living.*
> *But the child that is born on the Sabbath day*
> *is fair and wise and bonny and gay.*

TILL DEATH DO US PART

A long and happy future together or a lifetime of misery? The future fortune of a bride and groom may be determined by something as arbitrary as a cat sneezing near the bride on her wedding day (good luck) or a bride or groom singing (bad luck). As for rain on the wedding day ... that depends on whether or not you brought an umbrella.

A Sweep Is as Lucky as Lucky Can Be

In England, it's considered lucky to see a chimney sweep on your wedding day. In recent years, wedding planners have cashed in on this superstition by hiring out chimney sweeps—or people dressed as chimney sweeps—to attend weddings. But brides who can't afford one may be in luck regardless. According to the National Chimney Sweeps Association in London, high home heating prices bring a boon of luck for brides. When oil costs rise, more people purchase wood and turn to their fireplaces for heating. That leads to an increased need for chimney sweeps and a better likelihood of running into a real one on wedding day.

"Jumping the broom" is a common African-American tradition with its roots in an old superstition. Africans who came to the New World as enslaved people brought this tradition with them from their old countries. The broom is said to sweep away negativity and the old life. While living in slavery, jumping over the broom in itself constituted a legal marriage.

Something Borrowed, Something Blue

A bride should have "something old, something new, something borrowed, something blue, and a sixpence in her shoe" according to an English superstition. The rhyme, which dates to the 16th-century, can be interpreted to mean that the bride should have something that reminds her of her family (something old), something that symbolizes she's starting a new family (usually a ring), something to signify her fidelity (true blue), and the sixpence for good fortune. The superstition came to North America with settlers from the British Isles. Does following the custom work? A recent British bride told reporters that despite having all these lucky tokens, the wedding limousine carrying her groom and his mother crashed just yards from the church. The groom suffered through the ceremony with injuries to his back, arm, and leg, but his elderly mother had to be rushed to the hospital immediately after suffering a heart attack in the accident.

It's Like Rain on Your Wedding Day

Rain on a wedding day—good luck or bad? It depends on where you live. In many Spanish-speaking and Asian cultures, wedding day rain is considered good luck—it portends the many children that will come from the marriage. In other cultures, the rain is supposed to represent the tears that the bride will cry during her marriage.

In Brooklyn, New York, a couple celebrating a wedding at a hotel got an unexpected shower when the hotel's sprinkler system turned on just as the bride approached the altar. Guests on either side of the aisle were soaked before the system could be shut down. Although the couple, who are Russian immigrants, said that rain on your wedding day is considered good luck in Russia, they still sued the hotel for $300,000.

During a drought in Bangalore, India, a wedding was staged for two donkeys in the hopes that, according to an old superstition, such an event would bring rain. In another area of the country, a couple of frogs got hitched for the same reason.

Blackening the Bride and Groom

In the Orkney Islands, there's an old tradition of "blackening" the groom, which is similar to a fraternity hazing ritual. The unsuspecting groom is ambushed by friends who attempt to get him as messy as possible by throwing eggs, flour, oil, and feathers at him, and then they load him in a truck and drive

Not going to win best dressed, am I!?

around town, making noise and calling as much attention to him as possible. Historians think the practice has its roots in preventing an abduction of the groom by fairies, who will be scared away by the noise. Others say it's a precursor to the washing ritual a groom is supposed to go through—he should be really dirty before getting really clean. On mainland Scotland, the bride is also blackened.

Out of Sight

In many European cultures, it's considered unlucky for the groom to see the bride in her gown before she arrives at the ceremony. Some superstitions even say that the groom can't see her at all in advance—in the dress or not—and others say that a bride must see the groom before he sees her. In a strange twist on the bride-and-groom-seeing-each-other superstition, a New York man was arrested for being too close to his bride after his wedding. The couple had been previously married to each other and while they were getting divorced, the wife had taken out a restraining order on him. They reunited and remarried. When a fight broke out at their reception, police recognized the man and arrested him for violating the restraining order which was still in place.

With This Collar, I Thee Wed

In a rural village in India, a two-year-old boy was married to a dog in a ceremony attended by most of the village. The bride, dressed in a yellow sari, was a six-month-old mutt called Jyoti. Villagers said it was not the first time that a male baby had been wed to a female dog—it's a traditional reaction to a superstition. The boy had grown a tooth on his upper gum, and that was seen as a bad omen of an attack by an animal such as a tiger. Marriage to a dog is said to ward off such an attack. After the ceremony, a feast was held for the guests. The bride ate pieces of bread and mutton while the groom had a bottle of milk. The boy's parents said they would look after their new daughter-in-law, but when

. . . For richer for poorer, in sickness and in health,
till fleas us do part.

their son is ready to marry a human, he will be able to do so without seeking a divorce. Just for the record, Indian law does not legally recognize marriage between humans and animals.

In Bangladesh, a wedding between two sacred trees was attended by 1,000 people who hoped that the ceremony would put an end to the local misfortune being caused by the evil eye. The trees—a banyan and a peepul, which grow side by side—were decorated with marigold garlands and red cloth for luck.

The Corpse Brides

According to a superstition called *minghun* that exists in rural northern China, it's bad luck for a man to die single. Single ghosts will haunt the dreams of the living and prevent their children from achieving prosperity. In order to send bachelors into the afterlife with better luck, families will conduct corpse weddings for recently deceased single sons and even find for them "ghost brides" so the sons may go to the afterlife as part of a couple and the families can avoid the hauntings. The custom is illegal, but persists nonetheless. In recent years, the shortage of living women in China (due to the one child policy and selecting the sex of the baby) has also resulted in a lack of ghost brides. In 2007, a corpse trader was arrested for killing six women to serve as corpse brides and selling their bodies to the families of recently deceased bachelors. The same year, five men were arrested for digging up the grave of a recently deceased teenaged girl and attempting to sell her as a corpse bride. The men selected her because people are willing to pay more for a young and more recently deceased woman than one who has been dead for some time.

All in the Timing

Those superstitions about proper days and times to do things of course extend to weddings, too. According to English superstition, weekend weddings are doomed:

> *Monday for wealth,*
> *Tuesday for health,*

Wednesday the best day of all,
Thursday for losses,
Friday for crosses,
Saturday for no luck at all.

The English also have a rhyme about the correct month to marry:

Married when the year is new,
he'll be loving, kind and true.
When February birds do mate,
you wed nor dread your fate.
If you wed when March winds blow,
joy and sorrow both you'll know.
Marry in April when you can,
joy for maiden and for man.
Marry in the month of May,
and you'll surely rue the day.

175

Marry when June roses grow,
over land and sea you'll go.
Those who in July do wed,
must labor for their daily bread.
Whoever wed in August be,
many a change is sure to see.
Marry in September's shrine,
your living will be rich and fine.
If in October you do marry,
love will come but riches tarry.
If you wed in bleak November,
only joys will come, remember.
When December snows fall fast,
marry and true love will last.

THE END IS NEAR

The preface to the last chapter of life starts with a long list of superstitions. While no one can really predict when the

Grim Reaper will come knocking, no one ever stops trying to determine when and where he'll show up next. Superstitions are just one way to try to exercise a little more control over the great unknown and maybe to stave off the inevitable for a little while longer.

The Omen

Crows are probably the most universal harbingers of death. Going all the way back to ancient Greece, seeing a crow nearby meant that someone would soon die. In the Middle Ages, crows were thought to be witches' helpers. and it was also believed that the devil could turn himself into a crow. In many cultures, a dog howling for no reason portends death. Dogs are thought to have a sixth sense that picks up on the presence of the spirit of death.

A bird flying into a house is seen as an omen of death in some cultures, but in others, the bird has to knock into a window and die for it to be a bad sign. In some parts of England, a robin flying through an open window portends death, but in other areas, watch out if a robin perches on the back of a chair. The person who most recently occupied the chair will die.

An owl appearing in the daytime is said to foretell death in many cultures. In Kenya, owls at any time of day are associated with death.

A white moth is considered to be an omen of death in some European and East Asian cultures. Because of its markings—which resemble a skull and crossbones—the rare death's head hawk moth caterpillar is thought to bring bad fortune and death. The creature was featured in the movie *The Silence of the Lambs.*

In one Rhode Island nursing home, the presence of a cat

I've got more lives left than you do, cat!

called Oscar is said to portend the death of a patient. The "cat of doom" was reportedly present at the death of twenty-five patients in two years. His record even called the attention of the *New England Journal of Medicine*. Not to be outdone by a cat, there's a dog called Scamp at an Ohio nursing home who is supposed to have the same skill, but a better record. According to the staff, the dog only barks when a resident is near death, and has predicted the passing of nearly forty residents.

Not all omens relate to animals. If a picture or a mirror falls off a wall, for no apparent reason it's said that someone will soon die. In Greece, if a clock that didn't work suddenly chimes, death is near. In some cultures, the clock must be stopped at the moment someone dies.

In 19th-century Europe and North America, a black cloth would be placed over all mirrors in the house because mirrors were said to hold the soul's reflection, and if a ghost sees its reflection, it will stay in the house.

Visions

It's said the President Abraham Lincoln had seen his own death in a dream. Lincoln, who openly talked about the visions he saw in his dreams, had dreamt of seeing a dead body wearing a shroud in the East Wing of the White House. When he asked the soldier guarding it who was under the shroud, the soldier replied that it was President Lincoln, who had been assassinated.

The Cry of the Banshee

In Ireland, the most common superstition about death is that the mythical banshee cries before someone in the house is about to die. A banshee is a female spirit who is typically only heard and not seen, and only certain people in a family are born with the gift of being able to hear her. Sometimes

181

it's said that the banshee only cries for members of the oldest Irish ruling families. Most describe the cry as a long, sorrowful wail.

Road Rage

Zimbabweans living near a stretch of road that's seen numerous fatal accidents in recent years say that the crashes are caused by the angry spirits of ancestors who have not been appeased lately because people have neglected traditional rituals. The area was the site of a car crash that killed the wife of Prime Minister Morgan Tsvangirai in 2009 as well as numerous other crashes. It's said that drivers on the road often see figures crossing the road that cause them to swerve and lose control of vehicles. The figures, they say are actually ghosts. Some blame the accidents on a much more practical issue: the country's economic and infrastructure collapse. Leaders in the area say that in the past, villagers would brew beer, beat drums, and slaughter animals to appease the spirits, but that the ritual has not been done in recent years due to migration into urban areas. They said they planned a cleansing ritual that they hoped would satisfy the ancestors and bring an end to the misfortune.

Endless Sleep

In some areas of the American South, it's said that if you sleep in the moonlight, you may soon never wake up again.

In Japan, you must never sleep with your head facing north. That's the position in which bodies are placed in a coffin, and if you sleep that way, you will soon die.

Burying The Dead

One shouldn't look into the eyes of a dead person because they may try to take you along with them. In 19th-century Europe and America, coffins were taken out of the home feet first in case the dead person would rise and try grab a living person to take along with him.

In European cultures, you should hold your nose while walking past a cemetery in case a ghost should try to possess you through this opening.

In Japan, superstition dictates that you should hide your thumbs when a funeral goes by or death will soon come to you or your parents.

In Indonesia, you shouldn't look at a coffin as it's being lowered into the ground—doing so will cause serious illness. Those who accompany a coffin to its burial place should wash their faces so that the spirit won't be able find them later and follow them around.

In some parts of Nigeria, it's believed that the more you spend on a funeral, the more the spirit of the deceased will reward you.

Can you hear me now?

Cell Service from the Grave

In South Africa, superstitious people have started a new trend of being buried with their cell phones. The practice started from the belief that witches or wizards can put people into a death-like sleep, creating a widespread fear of being buried alive. With a cell phone at the side of the deceased, loved ones can be assured that if the family member is not actually dead, but only in a trance, he or she will be able to make a call from the coffin upon waking. The practice has now spread to other countries, including Ireland, Australia, Ghana, Chad, and the US. Most families now request that the cell phones be turned off so that the batteries won't be drained.

The Hmong of Laos and Cambodia believe that a picture of a person should not be buried or the person's soul will exit his or her body. A Minnesota school teacher who worked with Hmong children died and was buried with a picture of her class. Parents of the students later insisted that the body be exhumed and the photo removed from the coffin because they feared that keeping it there was putting their children's souls in jeopardy.

Born Again

In Thailand, people wishing for a fresh start in life have started "dying" for a few minutes as a way to put their problems behind them. A Buddhist monastery offers people a chance to "sleep" in a pink coffin for five minutes while the monks pray over them to cleanse their souls. Thousands of Thai people have taken advantage of the opportunity, paying the equivalent of $5 for a renewal of their karma without having to actually die first to get it.

Feed the Ghost

In China and south Asian countries with many Chinese immigrants, the Festival of the Hungry Ghosts is held on the fourteenth day of the seventh month of the lunar calendar. The timing coincides with the days when the doors of heaven and hell are said to be open, allowing ghosts to return to Earth for a short time. During the festival, spirits that did not receive a proper burial come back to Earth, and must be appeased lest they exact vengeance on the living. People prepare meals and leave an empty seat at the table for the spirits. They're offered items that they might need in the afterlife such as pajamas, television sets, and even "hell money" all made out of paper. People row out to sea with offerings for those who were drowned at sea, but it's not advisable to go swimming during this time—the spirits might drag you down with them. On the final evening of the festival, bonfires are held for all the paper items and the spirits are escorted back to where they came from. The hope is that the spirits will be satisfied enough to leave the living alone. The Hungry Ghost Festival bears some similarities to ancestor festivals in other cultures, such as Mexico's Day of the Dead, Japan's Oban Festival, and All Soul's Day in Europe.

Index